Emotional Brandywine

Paintings by Karl J. Kuerner

With Essays by Bruce E. Mowday

Berkeley, California

Emotional Brandywine
Copyright © 2023 by Bruce E. Mowday & Karl J. Kuerner
All rights reserved.

Published by Regent Press, Berkeley, California

Printed in the United States of America by
DavCo Advertising, Inc., Kinzers, Pennsylvania 17535

No part of this book may be used or reproduced in any manner whatsoever without written permission except in the case of brief quotations.

For more information, address Bruce E. Mowday
160 Chandler Drive, West Chester, PA 19380

Book Design by Leslie Steele
Cover Art by Karl J. Kuerner

Library of Congress Control Number

ISBN 13: 978-1-58790-665-7
ISBN 10: 1-58790-665-1

Dedication

This book is dedicated to those brave Patriots who fought and died at
Brandywine and contributed to emotions felt there today.
May they never be forgotten.

Contents

Dedication 7

Acknowledgments 11

Foreword 13

Birmingham Meeting Fog 16

Introduction 17

The Silent Drummer 20

Vision of Freedom 22

Philadelphia Campaign 24

Brandywine Flag 26

Moonlight on the Brandywine 28

Flintlock 30

Go Fish 32

Fording the Brandywine 34

The Soldier Left Behind 36

Barber House 38

Footnote 40

The Lafayette Sword 42

Thinking Bench 44

Tricorn	46
When Crows Fly By	48
Dawn's Early Light	50
Brinton House	52
The Brandywine Hills	54
Brandywine Retreat	56
A September Past	58
Ever Skyward	61
Index of Paintings	63

Acknowledgments

Books are the product of the efforts and support of many people. Karl and Bruce thank everyone who helped with *Emotional Brandywine*.

Part of the *Emotional Brandywine* team, including Shay Aubrey Allen and Simsun Greco, assisted in the *Emotional Gettysburg* book published by Regent Publishing. Shay contributed insightful thoughts and viewpoints for the studies of the paintings created by Karl. Shay also created the drawings of the authors used in the biographical section. Likewise, Simsun offered great insights and support in connection with the essays written by Bruce.

In any book, the publishing phase can be lengthy and challenging. For *Emotional Brandywine*, the publishing was smooth. Clair Leaman of DavCo Advertising used his experience and expertise to guide the book through design and printing. Publisher Mark Weiman of Regent Press was supportive of both of Karl and Bruce's books, *Emotional Brandywine* and *Emotional Gettysburg*. Proofreader Mary Walsh, also an author, did an excellent job. Jane E. Dorchester, Architectural Historian, provided research. Frank Davis assisted with the photographic transfer of Karl's paintings to the book designer.

Brandywine holds a special place in the history of the United States. Persons dedicated to preserving the region's history greatly helped in the production of *Emotional Brandywine*. Randell Spackman is one such individual. He owns Thornbury Farm. Randell's family property was part of the fiercest fighting during the afternoon of September 11, 1777. Randell's expertise was utilized in Karl's paintings and Bruce's essays.

The Religious Society of Friends, the Quakers, was kind enough to open the Old Kennett Meeting House for Karl and Bruce. Lars Farmer, Clerk of the Old Kennett Committee, gave a private tour of the Meeting House. The first shots of the Battle of Brandywine were fired outside the Meeting House.

Osborne Hill was an important location in the Battle of Brandywine. Brothers Richard and Philip Moore, owners of the property, allowed Karl and Bruce access to the location where British generals William Howe and Charles Cornwallis prepared their troops to attack General George Washington's soldiers on Birmingham Hill.

The Brandywine Conservancy and Museum of Art's preservation of Birmingham Hill was utilized in Karl's painting *Lafayette's Sword*. The preserved land is the location where General Lafayette, an American hero, was wounded late in the afternoon of the battle.

Foreword

For me, the book *Emotional Brandywine* began in the 1970s. I came to this realization while completing paintings for this book. My journey to depict the American Revolution's Battle of Brandywine started when I first created paintings of the Brandywine and appreciated the area's rich history. This book is the culmination of my life experiences living and painting on the battlefield and around Chadds Ford.

Being born and raised in the heart of the Brandywine Valley, I realize the area is so inspirational. This is my home.

I remember the 200th anniversary celebration of the Battle of Brandywine in 1977. I was 20 years old. There was a battle reenactment taking place and several of my friends and I walked to the event, which was being held behind the old Chadds Ford gallery, now closed. I said I knew a shortcut and we crossed through a cornfield. We came to an opening and there, to my surprise, were British soldiers. To say I was startled is an understatement. That encounter took me back to the time of the battle. I could imagine local farmers and their families at the time meeting British and American soldiers as the battle raged around them.

Many of the people now residing here don't realize the sacrifices made on these hills for all of our freedom. The culmination of the day's engagement on September 11, 1777, was not a grand victory but the bravery of the Americans laid the foundation for our freedom. Too many people today take our freedom and independence for granted. Those Americans should visit Brandywine as the spirit of those soldiers lingers on the battlefield.

I grew up on what is now known as Kuerner's Hill. Betsy Wyeth, Andrew's wife, told me that during the battle, town residents gathered on the hill to watch General John Armstrong's Pennsylvania militia defend the Brandywine River at Pyle's Ford and to view the day's fighting on other sections of the battlefield.

I've found musket balls on my family's fields. The day's battle had skirmishes throughout the area. Soldiers defended their liberty on this property and elsewhere, away from the main engagements of the day. One year, we plowed the fields behind the old Chadds Ford post office, now closed, in preparation for planting corn. After rain storms we would return to see if any artifacts had risen to the surface. We found musket balls. There had to be fighting in those fields.

Kuerner's Hill has witnessed so much history through the years. None has been as emotional as the Battle of Brandywine where Americans fought for freedom.

Karl J. Kuerner
July 2023

Birmingham Meeting Fog

Introduction

Walking through the fields of the Brandywine battlefield, one can't help but experience a variety of emotions.

The strong feelings emanating from the hallowed ground of Brandywine are the foundation of *Emotional Brandywine*. On September 11, 1777, brave American patriots fought with General George Washington to defend the young nation's capital of Philadelphia.

The day was long for the American soldiers. The British army of generals William Howe and Charles Cornwallis outflanked Washington's troops and came close to capturing the American army. Indeed, several British officers wrote that if they had several more hours of daylight that day, Washington's army would have ceased to exist.

American heroes saved the day. Individual soldiers bravely opposed England's professional army. General Anthony Wayne contested the crossing of the Brandywine by British troops. The soldiers of generals Nathanael Greene and Adam Stephan stymied the British late in the day, thus allowing Washington to guide his troops to safety that evening in Chester, Pennsylvania.

In the field west of the Birmingham Meeting House, a young and unknown Frenchman fearlessly dismounted and rushed to the front of an American unit to rally the troops. He was shot in his left leg as British soldiers advanced upon this position.

The Frenchman, who celebrated his 20th birthday five days before the battle, survived and went on to become an American hero. The Marquis Lafayette was instrumental in winning the American Revolution. His rise to the status of hero began when he was wounded on the field at Brandywine.

As the American Friends of Lafayette believe, Lafayette is the story of Brandywine.

The inspiration for *Emotional Brandywine*, as well as the companion book *Emotional Gettysburg*, came from renowned Brandywine artist Karl J. Kuerner. Karl was personally guided in fine art by Carolyn Wyeth and her brother Andrew Wyeth, world famous for his insightful renderings of life. Karl is the only artist personally tutored by Carolyn and Andrew, children of world-class artist and illustrator N. C. Wyeth.

The series of paintings Karl created for *Emotional Brandywine* has many of the fine nuances of a Wyeth painting plus Karl's own distinct artistic qualities. The essays are authored by Bruce E. Mowday, who has written more than 20 books on history, true crime, business and sports. He was authored three books on Gettysburg and *Emotional Brandywine* is his third book on Brandywine.

After the publishing of *Emotional Gettysburg* in 2019, Karl and Bruce decided their next project would be Brandywine. Both artist and author grew up near the Brandywine battlefield. Karl's family property, as is his home, is on a segment of the massive battlefield where skirmishes took place. Bruce is a past president of the Brandywine Battlefield Park Associates.

Karl created a series of paintings combining today's scenes with a sense of history.

Karl and Bruce spent hours walking the battlefield. They explored the ground where Lafayette was wounded and Sandy Hollow where Americans fought bravely to delay the advancing British. Two Quaker meeting houses, Old Kennett and Birmingham, stood during the battle and survive today. Karl and Bruce took tours of each one.

Standing where American heroes stood facing their British foe can be solemn, as one recalls heroic deeds. Also, the recollections are emotional.

"This book is driven by emotion," Karl said.

Emotional Brandywine

The Silent Drummer

A solitary drummer silently gazes across the field of Sandy Hollow. The cacophony of chaos – the roar of cannons, the retorts of muskets, the frantic signals of drums and the anguish cries of the wounded soldiers – are a faint remembrance.

During the late afternoon of September 11, 1777, American soldiers hurried to gain defensive formations at Sandy Hollow to stop the onslaught of the British army. On from Osborne Hill, across Street Road, past the Birmingham Meeting House steadily marched the American foes towards Sandy Hollow.

Even though the British army drove the Americans from the field that day, Washington's troops delayed the British advance long enough to allow the Colonial army to survive to not only fight another day, but win freedom for the 13 colonies.

Karl's inspiration for the painting came after a Brandywine reenactment on the field in September 2022. Almost 1,000 re-enactors spent two days at Sandy Hollow giving 10,000 spectators a glimpse of the camp life, hardships and battle conditions of a soldier during the American Revolution.

"After the reenactment, I went to the field and I heard the quiet," Karl said. "No fifes, or carriages, or sounds of battle. Just solitude. The solitude of freedom. Each soldier fought for individual rights.

"The sight was moving. The brilliant color of the sunset added to the scene. I could then hear the sounds of the one drummer echoing through the valley, signifying what took place that afternoon."

One of Karl's friends is quite the drummer. Karl plans to join that friend on the field and hear the cadence of a lonely drum, echoing across the field where a major historical event in our nation's history took place.

For Bruce, Sandy Hollow and Thornbury Farm are twins. When Bruce researched his book September 11, 1777: Washington's Defeat at Brandywine Dooms Philadelphia, the first on the Battle of Brandywine, Thomas Spackman gave Bruce a personalized tour of his Thornbury Farm property. For *Emotional Brandywine*, Tom's son Randell did the honors. Randell proudly proclaims America's rich history every chance he receives.

British officers wrote after the battle that if they had two more hours of daylight, they would have captured Washington's army. Upon the ground at Sandy Hollow, brave Americans fought and died to deprive the British of the time to conquer Washington's army.

Vision of Freedom

*I*n the early morning hours of September 11, 1777, a portion of the British army under Hessian General Baron Wilhelm von Knyphausen marched from the little village of Kennett Square.

Knyphausen received clear instructions. His troops must force the Americans on the western side of the Brandywine River back across the waterway and keep Washington's forces at bay until British generals William Howe and Charles Cornwallis outflanked the Americans. When the flanking maneuver was completed, both sections of the British army were to advance and catch Washington in a deadly trap.

One of the first clashes that morning took place just outside the walls of the old Kennett Meeting House. Knyphausen's troops faced the command of American General William Maxwell. As the skirmish developed, members of the Society of Friends, the Quakers, worshiped inside the building.

Quaker Jacob Pierce recalled, "While there was much noise and confusion without, all was quiet and peaceful within." True to their beliefs, the Kennett Square Quakers eschewed the war, even when the conflict was at their front door.

The Quaker Meeting House appears in many paintings. Most of the views depict the outside of the building. Karl and Bruce received a private tour of the interior. Since the building is only open a few Sundays during the year, the tour was special for the artist and author.

"The essence of the painting is not the image of the young woman looking out the window," Karl said. "She is looking out at the fighting and wondering what the future will bring to her and the nation. Will there be freedom? Will we remain subjects of the King of England? There is a sense of anticipation and wonder. Those within the Meeting House that day didn't know what was in store for the nation."

Karl chose to depict the Meeting House from the inside because the historical integrity of the Meeting House interior is maintained. The outside of the building has changed over the years. While taking the tour, Karl and Bruce had a chance to walk around the upper stories of the building.

"To get that ethereal, spiritual feeling, I painted from above the young woman as she looked out the window. Was she watching in wonderment or anticipation? This is so much more than a painting of someone looking out a window."

The fighting at the Old Kennett Meeting House didn't last long as the American soldiers retreated to the banks of the Brandywine and the British soldiers followed. Not all were able to continue. The graveyard of the Meeting House became the final resting place for soldiers of both armies.

Philadelphia Campaign

Farmers, merchants and shopkeepers populated George Washington's army. A scant number of professional soldiers held positions in the Continental army during the Philadelphia campaign of 1777.

The model for Karl's Philadelphia Campaign encompasses the attributes of those citizen-soldiers.

For years, Tom Stolfi was a dedicated staff member of the Brandywine Battlefield Park Associates. After viewing a reenactment, Karl selected Tom to represent the brave common soldier because of Tom's sense of fortitude and determination. Bruce was a board member of the park associates when he met Tom.

In good weather and during storms, Tom stood ready to give a glimpse of history to those visiting Brandywine Battlefield Park. Tom did so despite being hampered by the loss of one of his legs.

In Karl's portrait, Tom stands in front of a full moon and Philadelphia's Independence Hall. Philadelphia was the goal of the British troops under the command of General William Howe. The year before Howe was directed by his superiors in London to capture the capital city of the rebels, Philadelphia.

Washington recognized his citizen-soldiers were a poor match for the trained professionals in Howe's army. Washington couldn't avoid a full-scale battle, as Congress ordered Washington to not give up Philadelphia without a fight.

Behind the Brandywine River at Chadds Ford, Washington prepared his troops to meet the British.

September 11, 1777, did not go in Washington's favor. The Americans abandoned the field with heavy losses. The British possessed Philadelphia after American defeats at Paoli and Germantown.

Washington's citizen-soldiers survived the campaign and camped at Valley Forge that winter. Help soon arrived. Baron Von Steuben spent months drilling those farmers, merchants and shopkeepers into professional soldiers.

"We are going to prevail," was the message on Tom's face in the Philadelphia Campaign, according to Karl. Behind the eastern banks of the Brandywine River on September 11, 1777, a banner, destined to be known as the Brandywine flag, flew.

Brandywine Flag

Captain Robert Wilson's company in the 7th Pennsylvania Regiment carried the flag into battle. Part of General Anthony Wayne's command at the Battle of Brandywine, Wilson's men defended the river late in the afternoon as Hessian General Baron Wilhelm Knyphausen forced a crossing with his British army troops.

The 7th Pennsylvania resisted the British advance and then retreated to Chester, Pennsylvania, with the rest of George Washington's army. The Brandywine flag is believed to have been flown at other battles in the Philadelphia campaign, including Paoli and Germantown.

The origin of the 7th Pennsylvania Regiment dates to January 4, 1776, when the unit was formed in Carlisle, Pennsylvania. The regiment served in several other battles before merging with the 4th Pennsylvania Regiment on January 17, 1781.

The flag, Karl believes, is historic and important, even though the flag played just a bit part in the battle. "Most people are just small players in the scheme of things. The same goes for the Brandywine flag. It might be little known in our history but it is a major player," Karl said.

Independence National Historical Park displayed the Brandywine flag and the United States Postal Service honored the flag with a 33-cent stamp in 2000 as part of the Stars and Stripes postal series.

The distinctive flag is red, with a red and white American flag image in the canton and uses a 4-5-4 star pattern. The Brandywine flag was not an official flag of Washington's army. The banner was a militia company's flag.

Indeed, the naming of the Brandywine flag came as the fledgling country was defining the official flag of the United States. A resolution on June 14, 1777, just months before the Battle of Brandywine, mandated the national flag as having 13 stripes and 13 stars, although the specific pattern of the stars was not specified.

As Karl's painting depicts, the Brandywine flag's place in history is secure. The flag survives and is proudly flown over the hills of the Brandywine battlefield.

Moonlight on the Brandywine

Most days and nights, the Brandywine River is a serene place.

Picnics are enjoyed on its grassy shores. Canoers ride its gentle current. Nature lovers observe the flora and fauna. And, artists utilize the scenic twists and turns of the Brandywine as subjects for artistic creations.

Was the river as serene on the evening of September 10, 1777?

"I imagined it was so nice and peaceful that night. Only the campfire lights and the insects disturbing the calm," Karl said. "The next day would be just the opposite, full of mayhem."

That evening General George Washington readied his forces for the expected onslaught by the British Army. Washington deployed his troops south of Chadds Ford under the command of General John Armstrong. His right flank was guarded by General John Sullivan.

The morning of September 11 saw Washington rushing up and down the river giving orders. Close by were members of his staff, including Alexander Hamilton and the Marquis Lafayette.

Late in the morning, a portion of the British army descended on Chadds Ford and the fighting increased. Captain Patrick Ferguson, a British officer in the van of his army, had an American officer in his gunsight that morning. He reported withholding fire as the brave American was only doing his duty. Many believe that officer was Washington.

At one point, Washington ordered his men to cross the Brandywine to challenge the British. He abruptly withdrew the order as he was worried about a trap.

The chaotic afternoon reached its pinnacle when Hessian General Baron Wilhelm von Knyphausen crossed the Brandywine and assaulted the defensive position of American General Anthony Wayne.

Calmness returned to the Brandywine on the evening of September 11, 1777. The American forces retreated to Chester, Pennsylvania.

"If only the Brandywine could reveal what it witnessed that day," Karl lamented. "The stories it could tell."

Flintlock

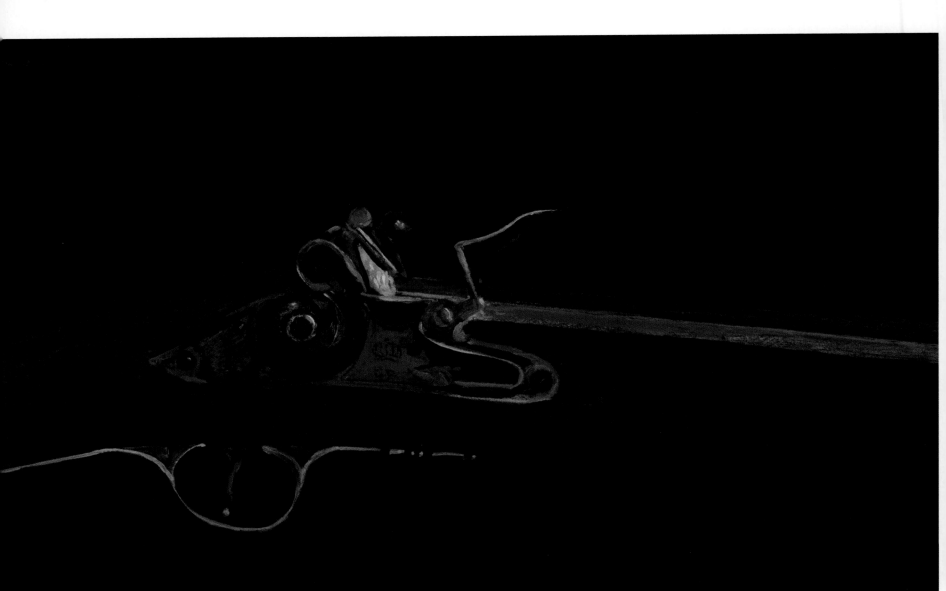

Weapons of war are equally monstrous and mysterious.

Each advancement in weaponry makes death and destruction easier to achieve. Sadly, military tactics are usually one war behind the development of weapons, leading to many unnecessary battlefield deaths.

Today's weapons are to be feared by every living creature on Earth. MAD – Mutually Assured Destruction – is more than a catchy phrase. Compared to the modern day drones, missiles and powerful bombs that threaten the survival of the world, the weapons of the American Revolution seem almost benign.

"The flintlock mechanism seems so primitive," Karl said. "How the structure worked fascinated me."

Even though the flintlocks, cannons and other military armaments used at Brandywine were primitive by today's standards, they were deadly. The total number of casualties during the day-long battle amounted to almost 2,000 men. Casualties include dead, wounded, missing and captured soldiers.

The British army kept better records than the Americans. British General William Howe's official tally recorded less than 600 casualties, including 93 killed and 488 wounded. General George Washington's army had imprecise accounts. The estimated American losses vary but most record between 200 and 300 American deaths, about 600 wounded soldiers and another 400 men missing.

The flintlock was developed in France in the early 17th century. Marin le Bourgeoys, an artist, gunsmith, luthier, and inventor from Normandy, is given credit for the design. The basic design became the standard for flintlocks, replacing older firing mechanisms. Flintlocks were used extensively until about the time of the American Civil War.

Flintlocks had a piece of flint held in place in between a set of jaws on the end of a short hammer. The hammer is pulled back into a cocked position before firing. Pulling the trigger releases the hammer, which swings forward causing the flint to strike a piece of steel called the frizzen. A cover is opened exposing gunpowder in a flash pan. The flint creates a spark and ignites the powder, resulting in the discharging of a projectile, such as a musket ball.

Go Fish

The stream banks of the Brandywine River at Jefferis' Ford today might not seem too different from the days before the armies of England and the United States clashed in Chester County.

"In many ways Jefferis' Ford has not changed at all," Karl said. "The area is beautiful and inspirational for artists. And, the Brandywine is still fished by man and bird to this day. The tranquility belies what took place here on September 11."

Indeed, the Brandywine River is a source of recreation in the 21st century. Previously, the waterway was used by the native population as a way to survive. Then, the Brandywine became part of the area's commerce as it was known as a river of mills in the 18th and 19th centuries.

After the American Revolution Battle of Brandywine became history and the mills no longer operated along the banks of the river, the populace of Chester County and surrounding areas used the Brandywine as a source of recreation.

Lenape Park provided amusement for several generations. The park was located between where General Washington's army prepared for the British and where William Howe and Charles Cornwallis, the British generals, outflanked Washington's troops.

For a time, steamboat rides, offered for 10 cents, ferried guests on the river at Lenape Park. Concerts took place and a fun house and merry-go-round were favored rides.

A triathlon began in the village of Marshallton and utilized the Brandywine as part of its competitive challenges. The river is part of the name of the Brandywine River Museum of Art, home to many of the paintings by the world-famous Wyeth family.

Picnics along the shores are common. Also, canoes are seen on the Brandywine during spring and summer days and nights. Bruce recalls filming a show for the Pennsylvania Cable Network outside of the Brandywine River Museum. Passing canoeists enjoying the river caused a brief halt to the filming.

For sure, with the crossing of about 6,000 members of the British Army there was no fishing by man or birds and no landscape painting taking place at Jefferis' Ford that September 1777 afternoon.

Today, the fishing has returned.

Fording the Brandywine

Fog shrouded the farmland of Chester County on the morning of September 11, 1777. Hot weather and recent rains caused the atmospheric conditions of that historic day.

British officers utilized the fog to help mask a flanking movement. More than 7,000 troops marched more than 14 miles from the town of Kennett Square to the high ground of Osborne Hill overlooking the rear of the American army.

Karl's painting incorporates the fog and the British army of generals William Howe and Charles Cornwallis. Howe's flanking maneuver was the same tactic he utilized the previous year when his English forces outflanked Washington on Long Island and won a major victory.

A key to Howe's plan was to have his army slip unnoticed around the right flank of Washington's defense along the Brandywine at Chadds Ford. Jefferis' Ford played an important role in the British plans. The ford was unguarded.

Washington was under the impression that the British could not move around the right of his forces because of the Brandywine. The British had better intelligence. Loyalists provided the British with a path that placed Washington's forces in danger of being captured.

That British path included crossing the Brandywine at Trimble's Ford and then Jefferis' Ford. The British army continued with their march to the heights of Osborne Hill where they formed for the attack on the rear of Washington's army.

Captain Friedrich von Munchhausen, aide de camp to General William Howe, wrote in his diary of the British Army's movement from Kennett Square, "At five o'clock in the morning General Howe marched off to his left ... we moved forward quickly in spite of the great heat. ... We crossed the Brandywine seven miles up from Chadds Ford, where the river is divided into two branches; the bridges were destroyed. The men had to cross these two branches in up to three feet of water. We then continued our march a short distance straight ahead, and then suddenly to the right down along the Brandywine toward the region of Chadds Ford."

One story related by Howard M. Jenkins in an 1877 article for Lippincott's Magazine had the British discovering liquor hidden by Wilmington merchants at Jefferis' Ford. "The casks were rolled out, the heads knocked in, and the officers, quaffing the old Madeira, drank to its rebel owners," Jenkins wrote.

If the British officers imbibed or not, they crossed the Brandywine at the two fords and successfully attacked Washington's army.

The Soldier Left Behind

Modern-day travelers on Birmingham Road, nearing the road leading to Radley Run Country Club, see a little sign designating the Osborne Hill property to the east as private.

On September 11, 1777, the land was possessed by an occupying British army under the command of General William Howe. From the hill, Howe directed the movements of his forces against those of General George Washington on Birmingham Hill.

Early in Karl's life, he became aware of Osborne Hill through a 1943 painting by Andrew Wyeth. When Karl met members of the Moore family, the current owners, he gained access to the views seen by Howe that afternoon of the American Revolution battle.

"What caught my attention was having the Moore family tell me of the property's history," Karl said. "At one time there was a body of a British soldier buried there but a former owner became freaked out over the remains on her property and had the soldier's body moved to a cemetery south on Birmingham Road, across from the Birmingham Meeting House."

While the battle took place during a bright, late-summer afternoon, Karl created his painting in early winter bleakness. "Just like the left behind British soldier, I could feel the aloneness of being forgotten. All of the troops have gone. The battles and war have long since subsided. The painting depicts that loneliness."

The Osborne Hill Farm was established in 1740, more than three decades before the Battle of Brandywine took place. Today, 88 acres of the Osborne Hill Farm are under a conservation easement, saving the land from being developed. The Osborne property contains farm fields and pasture, a stone farmhouse built in 1809, and about 30 acres of woodlands. Osborne Hill Farm was named for former owner Samuel Osborne who purchased the property in 1727.

"It's hard to imagine such a peaceful, beautiful spot being at the epicenter of the Revolutionary War's longest and largest battle," Natural Lands President Molly Morrison said at the time of the announcement of the easement. The farm was described as having the quintessential Chester County countryside of rolling fields, early 19th century buildings, and pastures.

Osborne Hill was by no means peaceful on September 11, as descriptions attested:

"At 4 p.m., with British regimental bands playing the *Grenadiers March*, Cornwallis struck the American right with fury." The assault was "the most Grand and Noble Sight imaginable."

Barber House

For many decades, a second battle of Brandywine has raged on the fields once occupied by brave soldiers of George Washington's army fighting the British military.

The battle's opponents are developers of large housing tracts and preservationists protecting historic land. The preservationists' victories include portions of Birmingham Hill, Sandy Hollow and Osborne Hill being placed under easement from development. The developers' wins are obvious by the many multi-dwelling housing developments on the battlefield.

Karl recalls being requested to paint a home near the Radley Run Country Club a number of years ago. The Barber House stood at the time of the Revolutionary War battle. The house continues to stand amidst many modern dwellings.

"I was told to forget the modern homes when I was asked to do the painting," Karl recalled. "I had to eliminate 250 years of growth to achieve the Colonial-era feeling."

The paintings for *Emotional Brandywine* were more challenging for Karl than *Emotional Gettysburg*.

"Brandywine is so different from Gettysburg," Karl said. "Gettysburg is preserved through the National Park Service. At Brandywine, there are no Devil's Den, no Little Round Top, no Wheatfield, and no Peach Orchard. Those places are so well-known at Gettysburg."

Gettysburg is easier for visitors to traverse than Brandywine, according to Karl. While Gettysburg has controlled park roads for visitors, at Brandywine country roads are bordered by busy routes 1 and 202.

Another element missing from Brandywine is the lack of individuals connected to the battle. "Tillie Pierce sparked my interest at Gettysburg," Karl said. "There are no Tillie Pierce personalities at Brandywine."

Pierce was a teenager during the Battle of Gettysburg and recorded her story in a book. The closest person Brandywine has is Joseph Townsend, a young Quaker man, who was at Osborne Hill amongst the British army and wrote about what he saw.

Both battles had famous people associated with the conflicts – Lincoln at Gettysburg and Washington and Lafayette at Brandywine – but Brandywine doesn't have a Tillie Pierce.

Footnote

*A*n iconic photograph exists of two famed Chadds Ford residents, Andrew Wyeth and Chris Sanderson. They sit on a bank overlooking Route 1. A Battle of Brandywine marker proudly stands in front of the pair.

Wyeth was a family member of the famed artist family that flourished in Chadds Ford and Maine. The Brandywine River Museum of Art in Chadds Ford features paintings by the Wyeths, including Andrew, his son Jamie and his father N. C. Sanderson was a local celebrity and character. He was a teacher, radio personality, historian and fiddle player. Many days, Sanderson hitchhiked to his destinations as he didn't drive. He lived on the battlefield before it became a state park and started the Chris Sanderson Museum in Chadds Ford. The museum houses historical gems and minutiae, including the photograph of Wyeth and Sanderson.

In recent years, different organizations erected a multitude of signs and markers identifying the Brandywine Battlefield. "The signs are here and there," Karl said. "Finding them is like taking part in an Easter egg hunt. You have to look for them. I found one by the Gables restaurant. I didn't know one existed there."

Living on a section of the battlefield, daily Karl passes the historical markers. "I never saw one person reading them," Karl said. "I'm sure some people do so. Brandywine plays such an important part in our quest for independence. It's sad to see people don't recognize or remember the sacrifices made at Brandywine."

Indeed, even though Brandywine was the largest land battle of the Revolutionary War and the main engagement of the Philadelphia Campaign, the battle has been lost in the fog of history. The documentaries and books on the Revolution usually give Brandywine brief, if any mention.

Bruce believes he discovered why Brandywine is overlooked. While researching his book *September 11, 1777: Washington's Defeat at Brandywine Dooms Philadelphia,* the first major accounting of the battle, Bruce spent time in London during research at the British Army Museum and the Public Records Office.

At the Public Records Office, akin to the National Archives, Bruce was told by the clerks that yes, they had heard of the American Revolution but weren't aware of the Battle of Brandywine.

Since the victors of the battle, England, lost the war, England doesn't dwell on the war and its victories. Since George Washington lost the battle for some of the same reasons he was defeated the previous year at Long Island, he didn't write about Brandywine.

Even though Brandywine was orphaned by the participants, the battle was so important to the gaining of freedom. That reason centered on a young Frenchman on Washington's staff, Lafayette.

The Lafayette Sword

One brief moment on Birmingham Hill marked the beginning of an American hero, the Marquis Lafayette.

Lafayette celebrated his 20th birthday five days before Brandywine. The engagement was Lafayette's first battle of the young general's life. As he was rallying troops of General Thomas Conway, a British musket ball wounded Lafayette in the left leg. When Lafayette spilled his blood in the American cause, he proved himself to George Washington, his fellow troops and the world that he was dedicated to the cause of freedom.

Karl and Bruce spent part of a fall afternoon walking on the ground where Lafayette was wounded. The field, now preserved by the Brandywine Conservancy, gave Karl a chance to view the site where a young Frenchman was willing to put his life on the line for American independence.

The overriding importance of Brandywine is Lafayette, representatives of the American Friends of Lafayette told Bruce as Bruce was researching his book *Lafayette at Brandywine: The Making of an American Hero*. Bruce was asked, "What took you so long at Brandywine to realize this? We've always known Lafayette's importance."

America desperately needed France's assistance to defeat England and Lafayette was a vocal proponent of America's independence. His lobbying helped gain France's aid.

Congress recognized Lafayette's importance to the cause of freedom. On August 24, 1779, Benjamin Franklin wrote to Lafayette, "The Congress sensible of your Merit towards the United States, but unable adequately to reward it, determined to present you with a Sword, as a small Mark of their grateful Acknowledgement."

Franklin's letter continued, "They directed it to be ornamented with suitable Devices. Some of the principal Actions of the War, in which you distinguished yourself by your Bravery & Conduct, are therefore represented upon it. These with a few emblematic Figures all admirably well executed, make its principal Value."

The sword was presented to Lafayette by Franklin's grandson, William Temple Franklin. Benjamin Franklin was ill at the time. Four battles that involved Lafayette were depicted on the sword, Monmouth Courthouse, Barren Hill, Gloucester and Rhode Island. On the sword, Lafayette is depicted slaying the British lion and America being released from its chains of imprisonment.

Five days after receiving the sword, Lafayette thanked Franklin for the "Noble present."

During the French Revolution and Lafayette's imprisonment in Austria, Adrienne Lafayette buried the sword for safekeeping. The blade rusted but the handle and mounting survived. The sword was smuggled to Lafayette by his son, George Washington Lafayette.

Thinking Bench

The Chester County Quaker community suffered during the Philadelphia campaign. Most members adhered to their strong belief of being neutral in the American War for Independence. Others, such as American General Nathanael Greene of Rhode Island who fought at Brandywine, did not follow the religion's non-violent vows.

Quaker farmer Gideon Gilpin and his family lived on the battlefield. His property was plundered by the armies fighting at Brandywine. His reported losses included:

- 10 "milch" cows
- 1 yoke of oxen
- 48 sheep
- 28 swine
- 12 tons of hay
- 230 bushels of wheat
- 50 pounds of bacon
- 1 history book
- 1 gun

General George Washington made his headquarters in the Benjamin Ring House, close to the Gilpin residence. Gilpin's home is known as Lafayette's headquarters. No verification exists concerning the young French general actually sleeping in the house and he didn't command troops at Brandywine. Lafayette did know Gilpin, no doubt. Lafayette's secretary recorded an eyewitness account of a joyful reunion between the two men during Lafayette's grand tour of the United States in July 1825.

The loss of personal property caused the Gilpin family financial hardship. As a result, a tavern was opened to earn money for Gilpin's family.

Karl selected a bench and a sycamore tree, a witness to the Battle of Brandywine, as subjects. The tree has been called the "Lafayette Sycamore" and tree experts estimate the tree is more than 250 years old.

A myth exists that Lafayette was treated for his leg wound under the tree. Lafayette was shot on Birmingham Hill, treated in the woods behind Wylie Road and then taken to Chester. By the time Lafayette was wounded, the area around the Gilpin home was being contested by the two armies. Another myth has Lafayette being treated at the Birmingham Meeting House. The Meeting House was in British control moments after Lafayette was wounded.

In 2019, Longwood Gardens planted a sycamore from the Lafayette tree. According to a Longwood publication, "Planted around 1730, the tree is often called the Lafayette sycamore, and towers at the southwest corner of the Gideon Gilpin House. Originally the home of a Quaker farmer, the house served as the quarters for the 20-year-old Frenchman Marquis de Lafayette, who saw his first military engagement in America, and was subsequently wounded, during the September 11, 1777 Battle of Brandywine."

tricorn

Tricorn hats were worn everywhere in the 18th century. The chapeaus came in many different styles and were made from different material. From aristocrats to the common working man, the tricorn was the hat of choice.

"Many of the American soldiers wore whatever they had. Many didn't have official uniforms," Karl said. "Those wearing tricorn hats at Brandywine could once have been a farmer or a shopkeeper or an elected official." The occupation didn't matter. "What is important is the spirit of the figure under that tricorn. This painting represents the spirit of the American soldier."

The hat was usually worn with one point facing forward, though some soldiers had their tricorn pointed to the left to allow better clearance for their musket. American soldiers' official uniforms varied. Some wore a vest-like waistcoat and a wool regimental coat. These outer coats could be dark blue, brown, or green. Colors distinguished everything from the state the soldier represented to rank to a soldier's unit.

The standard uniform of the British army also included a tricorn hat, at least at the beginning of the war. Later in the conflict, regiments replaced their tricorn hats with slouch hats. The remaining uniform consisted of the traditional red coats, white breeches and black gaiters with leather knee caps.

British Loyalist troops wore scarlet uniforms, similar to the British army regular soldiers. Hessian soldiers usually donned blue coats. Hessian Fusiliers, light infantry regiments, wore miter caps. The caps were unique. The brass finial, supports, and crown were stamped with a variety of military symbols. The brass cap plate had a Hessian lion. The lion was shown rearing on the left hind leg with the forelegs elevated. The head was in profile and holding a sword. The sword was engraved with the initials "FL" for *Friedrich Landgraf,* the ruler of Hesse-Cassel.

The term tricorn came about in the 1800s. At the time of the American Revolution, the hats were more commonly called "cocked hats." The hat's distinguishing characteristic was that three sides of the brim were turned up (cocked) and either pinned, laced, or buttoned in place to form a triangle around the crown.

French Musketeers wore the tricorn in the 17th century.

When Crows Fly By

Proudly standing, overseeing the Brandywine River, is a landmark home, the John Chads House. The Chadds Ford home, and its springhouse, come as close to being a monument as any structure on the Brandywine battlefield.

Over the decades, many paintings and photographs have featured the front of the historic home. Karl sought a different perspective for his painting. He decided to utilize the rear of the home for his creation.

The view Karl chose was the vision seen by American soldiers during the day of the battle, September 11, 1777. Indeed, young French General Lafayette wrote in his memoirs about being behind the home with General George Washington during the morning hours.

Washington placed the main body of his army on the eastern shore of the Brandywine to meet the mighty British army. Washington's artillery, planted on the hills behind the John Chads Home, traded rounds with the British cannons under the command of Hessian General Wilhelm von Knyphausen. One report states Elizabeth Chads remained in the home during the battle and observed the action from her attic window. Also, she placed her silver spoons in her pockets to keep them safe.

The home was constructed in the early 1700s, one date lists 1713, by John Chads. John Wyeth, Jr., no relation to the famous Wyeth artist family that later lived just north of the John Chad House, is given credit for designing the home. Chads began a ferrying service across the Brandywine in the 1740s. The ferry operated until the 1820s when a bridge was constructed across the Brandywine.

For a few years after the battle, the springhouse served as a schoolhouse. The property was privately owned until the Chadds Ford Historical Society took over the site in 1968 and did extensive renovations. The historical society's main building sits across Creek Road from the John Chads House. During Chadds Ford Days in September of most years, a beehive oven on the property, named for Elizabeth Chads, bakes bread for visitors.

The house was added to the National Register of Historic Places on March 11, 1971. The Pennsylvania Historical and Museum Commission recognized the home in 1915.

Dawn's Early Light

For more than a century, members of the Kuerner family have farmed the fields of Kuerner Hill.

"The vision continues," Karl said of his painting *Dawn's Early Light*. Not only does the coming day unfold before the hill, but also the history of Chadds Ford and the Brandywine Valley.

A significant part of the history includes the Battle of Brandywine. Neighbor Betsy Wyeth, wife of artist Andrew Wyeth, relayed a story to Karl concerning the hill and members of the Chadds Ford community. Betsy told Karl that members of the Chadds Ford community gathered on the hill to watch the historic engagement.

"Kuerner Hill has seen everything," Karl pronounced. "It has seen so much history."

The hill has produced solid evidence to support Karl's claim. Karl has found four or five musket balls fired during the Battle of Brandywine on the hills. "Something happened on that spot where those musket balls were discovered. You don't realize how extensive the battle was that day. Skirmishes took place throughout the area."

Karl recalls plowing the fields behind the old Chadds Ford post office, now closed, in preparation for planting corn. "After rain storms, we would return to see if artifacts had risen to the surface. We found musket balls. There had to be fighting in those fields."

Chadds Ford's rich farmland has surrendered many artifacts. Parts of Dutch pipes, popular during the 1700s, and other remnants from the battle surfaced and were discovered. Karl was shown a 1775 British coin discovered near nearby Ring Road after a rainstorm.

Being aware of history has assisted Karl in creating his paintings. "We weren't the first people here. The discovery of the artifacts feeds your creativity," Karl said. "If you know some of the history, your imagination will take you to another level. I then create these paintings. And, I hope these paintings will take others to the same place I experienced."

Soldiers defended their liberty on Kuerner's Hill. Those viewing Karl's paintings can experience the day brave Americans fought on Kuerner's Hill to gain our freedom and independence.

Brinton House

Location, location, location is so important, as Realtors like to say.

William Barns, a blacksmith in the early 1700s, saw a need for a tavern on "ye Great Road to Nottingham." At the time, the path was a major route from Philadelphia to Maryland.

The location Barns selected was in Pennsbury Township between the village of Kennett Square and Chadds Ford. He purchased property and completed construction in 1714.

The house was described by the Chadds Ford Historical Society, the current owners, as a "spacious brick building that was to become a tavern. With a diamond-patterned gable and Flemish bond brickwork accentuated with black headers, the handsome building was aptly fitted for use as a tavern. There was a private side for the Barns family and a barroom with sleeping quarters above for weary travelers.

"Further evidence of the building's use as a tavern exists in the cellar. There are a total of five niches in the foundation walls. They were used to keep 'bevriges' and foodstuffs cool."

From records, Barns began operating his tavern in 1722 for "yea accommodation of Man and Horse." Man and horse stopped at the tavern until at least 1726. Barns foresaw a need but was not a great businessman.

As the tavern delved deeper into monetary problems, a license renewal application was denied in 1728. Barns died in 1731, deeply in debt, according to written accounts.

The location was important during the Battle of Brandywine. British troops under Hessian General Wilhelm von Knyphausen surged past the former tavern on their way to confront General George Washington's troops behind the Brandywine River at Chadds Ford.

At the time of the battle, James Brinton was the owner of the house. He purchased the property in 1753. According to claims, the tavern suffered damage during the battle.

Karl said, "History brings along with it inspiration, imagination and contemplation of what is and what was. The Brinton house has seen so many changes since it was first built in 1714. The overwhelming thought that came to my mind was silence, especially in the evening, and, of course, solitude, waiting for the traveler to come by. The changes that were to come, would be a start of a new nation."

The Brandywine Hills

Except for the mercenary Hessian soldiers, British soldiers were fighting to preserve their country. They weren't invaders. They played a part in America's first great Civil War.

The regular Redcoats hailed from across the Atlantic Ocean. The army included loyalists from the colonies. In the American army were soldiers born in the United States but many of their officers were foreign born, including Lafayette and others at Brandywine.

Early in the war, British officers didn't pursue the American army as vigorously as they would later in the war. A mistaken belief was held that the Americans would come to their senses and remain loyal to the King.

At one point in the war, the British army reportedly had as many as 22,000 men in North America to suppress the rebellion. One report has 50,000 English soldiers fighting in America during the conflict. An additional 25,000 Loyalists, faithful to England's King, increased the size of the British army. An estimate of the number of Hessians taking part was 30,000.

The memory of the Redcoats is kept alive by re-enactors, including Randall Spackman. Spackman's property was part of the Brandywine battlefield, including Sandy Hollow. Randell and the other re-enactors meticulously research all aspects of British uniforms and weapons. Randell is the model for this painting.

"Having the opportunity to spend time with Randell was more than just painting sessions," Karl said. "It was a time to spend on the passion of local history which should be a national history. Randell's passion came through to me in his experiences as a re-enactor. He seems to fit the part of a British soldier. During our time together, Randell seemed to think he was one. To me, Randell's passion comes through in this painting."

Brandywine Retreat

*A*t the end of the long and frustrating day, the Battle of Brandywine was a major loss for General George Washington and his young band of Continental soldiers.

That evening, Washington approved a report to Congress from Chester. The account began, "I am sorry to inform you that in this day's engagement, we have been obliged to leave the enemy masters of the field."

Washington's report downplayed the number of men lost, writing that he believed the British army suffered more casualties than the Americans. In fact, Washington lost more than twice the number of soldiers than the English.

As for those injured and killed, Washington reported, "The Marquis de La Fayette was wounded in the leg, and Gen. Woodford in the hand. Divers other Officers were wounded some Slain, but the number of either cannot now be ascertained."

Congress, upon reading Washington's report, knew Philadelphia was lost. The seat of government was about to be moved to Lancaster and then on to York. Congress would not return until the next spring when the British army abandoned Philadelphia.

Despite the setback, Washington gave an upbeat report on the status of his soldiers. The report stated, "Notwithstanding the misfortune of the day, I am happy to find the troops in good spirits; and I hope another time we shall compensate for the losses now sustained."

Karl commented, "This painting was completed in 1979. I was 22 years old. Young artists sometimes try to romance history. I thank one can see Carolyn Wyeth's artistic influence in this piece. I added my own version to this sad part of the battle, possible casualties. The sacrifices our soldiers made were far more than most people realize."

A September Past

Centuries have come and gone since that day in 1777 when George Washington's soldiers fought for freedom against the British army under the command of General William Howe.

The battleground has changed in many ways. Fields once plowed by farmers, some by descendants of American Revolution soldiers, no longer provide crops for the community. Sadly, construction consumed historic ground.

In April 1840, noted Kennett Square author Bayard Taylor wrote about his first visit to the Brandywine River and the battlefield. His trek was made on "a lovely morning. Taylor wrote, "We came in sight of the Brandywine, flowing in placid beauty beneath the shade of tall trees which extended their long arms across, and, interlacing their boughs, seemed to form a protection. I thought what a contrast it presented to the turbid and crimsoned steam, which flowed upon the day of that ever-memorable battle."

Thousands of visitors a day pass through the battlefield. How many think about September 11, 1777? How many even know that a gallant stand by Washington's army took place? The cannon on Sandy Hollow marks the scene of some of the most ferocious fighting during the Battle of Brandywine.

One description of the area, now part of the Spackman property, reported a stream ran red with blood that afternoon. For several hours the opposing armies contested the land. The British goal was to destroy the rebel army once and for all and end the rebellion. The Americans fought for survival and to live to fight another day.

For those in touch with history, the land and the river provides reminders of the September long past. The land gives up artifacts of the battle. The river rolls past sacred ground where American soldiers lost their lives for freedom.

Even though many modern-day travelers might not be aware, the spirit of those patriots from a September long ago is alive.

Karl said, "Go to Sandy Hollow when no one is there. The quiet will take one back in time. It's harder to do now with more people living in the area, but on occasion you can hear the calmness."

Ever Skyward

Index of Paintings

A September Past: 1984, acrylic on panel 16 ½ by 47 ½" collection of Mr. Paul McLellan

Philadelphia Campaign: 2003, acrylic on panel 10 ¼ x 21 ½" collection of Mr. Paul McLellan

Brandywine Flag: 2022, acrylic on panel 24 x 30" private collection

Birmingham Meeting Fog: 2022, acrylic on panel 11 ⅞ x 19" private collection

Dawn's Early Light: 2001, acrylic on panel 48 x 96" private collection

Tricorn: 2022, acrylic on panel 16 ½ by 27 ¼" private collection

The Silent Drummer: 2022, acrylic on panel 29 ¾ x 39 ½" private collection

Barber House: 2022, acrylic on panel 23x 39" private collection

Moonlight on the Brandywine: 2022" acrylic on panel 21 by 40" private collection

Vision of Freedom: 2022, acrylic on panel 28 ¼ by 19" private collection

Footnote: 2022, acrylic on panel 18 ½ x 24 ½" collection the artist

When Crows Fly By: 2008, acrylic on panel 16 ½ by 24 collection of Mr. and Mrs. Brod Erb

Go Fish: 2021, acrylic on panel 31 ½ x 29 ½" collection the artist

The Soldier Left Behind (Osborne Hill): 2023, acrylic on panel 20 ½ x 38" private collection

Ever Skyward: 2021, acrylic on panel 32 x 49" private collection

Brinton House: 2023, acrylic on panel 22 ¼ x 15 ½" private collection

Brandywine Retreat: 1979, oil on panel 14 x 7 ½ private collection

Flintlock: 2022, acrylic on panel 5 x 7 ¼ private collection

Fording the Brandywine: 2022, acrylic on panel 8 ¼ x 6" private collection

The Brandywine Hills: 2023, acrylic on panel 17 x 32" private collection

The Lafayette Sword: 2023, acrylic on panel 9 ⅞ x 20 ⅞" collection the artist

Thinking Bench: 1988, acrylic on panel 8 x 13" collection of Mr. and Mrs. James A Nelson

Karl J. Kuerner

Karl was born in Chadds Ford, Pennsylvania on January 12, 1957 – to Karl and Margaret Kuerner – third generation farmers. His artistic talent was recognized and nurtured at a very young age by Carolyn Wyeth – sister of Andrew Wyeth and a renowned artist in her own right.

Kuerner grew up surrounded by artists and the task of painting. From the age of seven he watched Andrew Wyeth paint some of his greatest works at the Kuerner Farm – Karl's family homestead for three generations – and a major source of inspiration for more than 1,000 of Wyeth's works of art – and eventually over 300 of Kuerner's own works.

As Karl matured artistically, Andrew Wyeth took a keen interest in the young artist and took him under his wing – mentoring and teaching him for more than three decades.

"Wyeth looked at Karl Kuerner and said, 'It's up to you to carry this on. And it won't be easy'… Wyeth added, 'Karl understands what I'm about: pure, deep, emotion. I have always emphasized to Karl that an artist must paint what he loves… and Karl has been painting that which he loves for nearly forty years now. His work is inspiring and deeply introspective… it exhibits a strong honest quality that comes from deep within and touches the ordinary in a profound way."

Bruce E. Mowday

*B*ruce is an award-winning author and newspaper reporter. He has authored more than 20 books on history, sports, business and true crime. Mowday has appeared on numerous television and radio shows, including *Counter Culture*, a *PBS* Emmy-winning show, the *Discovery ID* channel, *ReelZ* network, *C-SPAN*, the *Pennsylvania Cable Network*, *Hollywood and Beyond*, *Our American Heritage*, *Whatcha Got*, *Journey into the Civil War*, *Chronicles of the American Civil War* and local television and radio stations.

He was a guest on the Massachusetts Historical Society's *Revolution 250*. He was twice featured in the Authors of the American Revolution Congress hosted by Nathan's Papers. Bruce is a frequent speaker at various civic and historical groups. The Congress of Civil War Round Tables has named Bruce a "5-Star" speaker. Mowday has hosted his own radio shows, has been an editor of magazines and was chairman of the Chester County Historical Society and president of the Brandywine Battlefield Park Associates. He is a former board member of the Valley Forge Park Alliance and the Chester County Conference and Visitors Bureau. For more information on Mowday, his books and his schedule of events, see www.mowday.com.

A member of the American Friends of Lafayette, Bruce is the Chester County Coordinator for the Lafayette Bicentennial Celebration in 2024 and 2025. He is also a member of the county's 250th committee planning for a celebration of our nation's founding.